EXPLORING
CAREERS

Careers in Renewable Energy

Don Nardo

ReferencePoint
Press

© 2018 ReferencePoint Press, Inc.
Printed in the United States

For more information, contact:
ReferencePoint Press, Inc.
PO Box 27779
San Diego, CA 92198
www.ReferencePointPress.com

Picture credits:
 6: Maury Aaseng
17: Shutterstock.com/Franco Lucato
25: iStockphoto/shotbydave
33: Caro/Oberhaeuser/Newscom
45: Max Whittaker/Reuters/Newscom

LIBRARY OF CONGRESS CATALOGING-IN-PUBLICATION DATA

Name: Nardo, Don, 1947– author.
Title: Careers in Renewable Energy/by Don Nardo.
Description: San Diego, CA: ReferencePoint Press, Inc., [2018] | Series: Exploring Careers |
    Includes bibliographical references and index.
Identifiers: LCCN 2017040868 (print) | LCCN 2017044876 (ebook) | ISBN 9781682823163 (eBook)
    | ISBN 9781682823156 (hardback)
Subjects: LCSH: Clean energy industries—Vocational guidance—Juvenile literature. | Renewable
    energy sources—Juvenile literature.
Classification: LCC HD9502.5.C542 (ebook) | LCC HD9502.5.C542 N37 2018 (print) | DDC
    333.79/4023—dc23
LC record available at https://lccn.loc.gov/2017040868

Contents

The Steady Rise of Green Energy Jobs

Renewable energy is also frequently called sustainable, green, alternative, or clean energy. Whichever name one chooses, it is a type of energy that can be used over and over again and will never be exhausted or run out. This is because it naturally replenishes itself and as a result does not need humans to replace it on a regular basis. Also, importantly, the various kinds of green energy do not damage the environment, as nonsustainable energy sources do. (The chief nonrenewable sources are the fossil fuels coal, oil, and natural gas.)

The most plentiful and perhaps best-known example of renewable energy is solar energy. Other major types of green energy include wind; geothermal (which utilizes the planet's inner heat); biomass (which is plant based), hydroelectric (which employs the energy of moving water); and nuclear (which taps the energy produced by radioactive elements).

A Rapidly Expanding Jobs Market

Like the fossil fuel industries, these green energy industries require the ongoing efforts of numerous scientists, technicians, managers, surveyors, installers, distributors, maintenance crews, and other kinds of workers. The renewable energy industries therefore support a large number of jobs. Moreover, they are currently the fastest-growing job-creating fields in the US economy.

In particular, in 2017 the solar and wind industries generated jobs at a rate twelve times faster than the economy as a whole. That year the Environmental Defense Fund (EDF), one of the world's largest nonprofit environmental organizations, published a comprehensive study of the growth of the green energy industry as a whole. It found that in recent years, careers in the solar and wind sectors worldwide had grown at the impressive annual rate of roughly 20 percent.

In actual job numbers, about 769,000 new green energy jobs were created globally in 2015 alone. By 2017 the world's renewable energy industries employed some 9.8 million people, up from 7 million in 2012. The United States' share in the global green jobs market is slightly less than a tenth—at just over 800,000. In marked contrast, between 2012 and 2017 jobs in coal mining and other fossil fuel industries registered an overall decline. US coal mining jobs, for example, fell from 150,000 in 1987 to about 51,000 in 2017. In a 2017 Climate Corps report, an EDF spokesperson states, "Not only is the renewable energy economy creating jobs faster than the fossil fuel industry, it also creates more jobs per dollar invested. For example, researchers at the University of Massachusetts Amherst estimate that investments in renewable energy generate roughly three times more direct and indirect jobs than comparable investments in fossil fuels."

One major reason for the recent dramatic rise in the numbers of green energy jobs has been a significant decrease in manufacturing and installation costs. For a long time the number of renewable energy jobs remained fairly low because those costs were high. As long as they remained high, the more cheaply produced fossil fuels were more popular, and the green energy industries grew very slowly at best. So growth in the number of workers in the sustainable energy fields remained fairly stagnant. When manufacturing and installation costs of green energy plummeted, however, solar, wind, and other renewables steadily became cheaper and more popular. In turn, the green energy industries needed to and did hire many new workers.

An often-cited example of those plummeting costs is solar panels. Each panel is made up of several dozen solar cells, each of which converts incoming sunlight into electricity. Producing a solar panel used to be extremely expensive, which explains why most people used oil and other fossil fuels instead of such panels to create electricity. In 1977 the production cost of making a solar panel was a whopping seventy-seven dollars for each watt of electricity the panel produced. By 2009, however, that cost had dropped to only seven dollars per watt; and by 2017 it was a mere sixty-four cents per watt. In forty years, therefore, the cost of making a solar panel plunged by an

Careers in Renewable Energy

Occupation	Minimum Educational Requirements	2016 Median Pay
Agricultural engineer	Bachelor's degree	$73,640
Atmospheric scientist, including meteorologist	Bachelor's degree	$92,460
Civil engineer	Bachelor's degree	$83,540
Computer programmer	Bachelor's degree	$79,840
Environmental engineering technician	Associate's degree	$49,170
Geoscientist	Bachelor's degree	$89,780
Hydrologist	Bachelor's degree	$80,480
Nuclear engineer	Bachelor's degree	$102,220
Nuclear technician	Associate's degree	$79,140
Line installer and repairer	High school diploma or equivalent	$62,650
Solar photovoltaic installer	High school diploma or equivalent	$39,240
Wind turbine technician	Technical school	$52,260

Source: Bureau of Labor Statistics, *Occupational Outlook Handbook*, 2017. www.bls.gov.

incredible 99.2 percent. This is one of the primary reasons why the solar industry is expanding rapidly and constantly hiring new people.

A Bright Future for Clean Energy

Renewable energy industry experts predict that the number of jobs in that economic sector will continue to rise in the coming years, reflecting a bright future for clean energy in general. Leading such forecasts is the International Renewable Energy Agency (IRENA), headquartered in Abu Dhabi, United Arab Emirates. IRENA expects the number of global green energy jobs to rise from just under 10 million in 2017 to at least 24 million by 2030.

Many US energy experts hope that their country will produce a hefty share of those future jobs. Some urge both government officials and private investors to go even further and allow the country to fulfill its huge technical, industrial, and economic potential. In theory, the United States could outproduce the rest of the world in renewable energy production and jobs, Vanderbilt University scholar and energy expert David J. Hess writes in the book *Good Green Jobs in a Global Economy: Making and Keeping New Industries in the United States*. If the nation "were to embark on a full-fledged green transition with an investment of $1 trillion," he points out in the book, the result would be the creation of "20 million to 30 million new green jobs."

Even if the federal government does not push for such an ambitious green energy jobs program, Hess and other authorities say, a similar goal may be attainable in a different way. Namely, it could happen through the cumulative effect of many individual states going increasingly green. A well-known example is California, which had the highest creation rate of solar power jobs of any US state in 2016. In 2009 the California Public Utilities Commission set a goal of making all homes in the state run at least partially on renewable energy by 2020. The commission's second goal is to have all the electricity used by commercial buildings in the state produced by green sources by 2030. Nevada, Hawaii, Vermont, and Massachusetts have also set ambitious sustainable energy goals.

One result of these efforts is sure to be the creation of many new green energy jobs. "Clean energy is no longer a niche business—it's a big-time job creator," says Dan Smolen, managing director of the Green Suits, a Virginia-based career development firm. His comments appear in a press release introducing the 2016 *Clean Jobs America* report by E2, a national nonpartisan group of business leaders and investors. In the same press release, Bob Keefe of E2 states that clean energy has become an important part of the US workforce and economy. "Smart policies helped jump-start this industry," he says, "and smart policies will keep these made-in-America jobs growing and help our environment along the way."

Solar Voltaic Designer

At a Glance
Solar Voltaic Designer

Minimum Educational Requirements
Bachelor's degree in engineering

Personal Qualities
Mechanically inclined, detail oriented, strong interest in science and math

Certification and Licensing
Required

Working Conditions
Mainly in offices, but with some travel to outdoor sites

Salary
About $90,000 per year on average

Number of Jobs
More than 260,000 solar industry workers in the United States in 2016*

Future Job Outlook
Thousands of new solar energy jobs projected to be created in the next few decades

*This number includes solar voltaic designers.

What Does a Solar Voltaic Designer Do?

Depending on the traditions of the region where they work and their exact duties, solar voltaic designers can be called by a number of other names. Some of these include solar thermal engineer, principal solar systems engineer, solar voltaic utility manager, solar voltaic systems engineer, and solar array engineer. The word *voltaic* in these job titles refers to the production of an electric current by chemical action, the process that happens on the surface of a solar panel.

One of the typical places where a solar designer works with such panels and other solar equipment is a solar farm. This is a large array of solar panels that gather sunlight, convert it to electricity, and send that energy to a nearby electrical grid for distribution to homes and businesses. On such a farm, a solar designer devises and develops the various components of the solar energy system, including the kinds of metals that will be used in the panels, how the panels will be set up, and how the system will operate. He or she also troubleshoots and corrects problems that may arise in the system. In some solar farms, the solar designer actually manages the entire site.

Only a few of the thousands of solar voltaic designers in the United States and other countries work on solar farms, however. Most of them work for solar companies that create and/or install solar energy systems for houses, businesses, factories, apartment buildings, and other venues. Usually, the designer's job begins with an inspection of the site where the solar energy system will be installed. He or she studies the structures and existing electrical systems and records the information on a computer. That data is then employed to design one or more solar-powered systems for the site. They may include an array of solar panels on the roof or elsewhere on the property, a space heating system, or a new hot water system. (Solar designers who specialize in heating and hot water systems are often called solar thermal designers or solar thermal engineers because the term *thermal* means "having to do with heat.")

Whichever kind of solar equipment will be installed on the site, the designer must initially decide how large the new system will be and how much energy it will produce, as well as how much energy it will require to operate. With the aid of a computer, he or she calculates all the data. Next the information is used to create technical diagrams that the installers will consult when they actually build the new system. The designer also often visits the site during the installation and oversees, directs, or otherwise supports the workers.

Solar designers' work may not be finished even after the installation is completed. They sometimes monitor the new system on a regular basis to make sure it is operating correctly. If it is not working as it should be, they determine what is causing the malfunction and fix it.

Many solar designers find great satisfaction in creating solar energy systems, in part because they enjoy the intellectual and mechanical challenges involved. Some say they are also motivated by the knowledge that the systems they design make people's lives better. Those systems usually save homeowners or businesses a considerable amount of money over time, for example.

Even more fulfilling for solar designers is bringing electricity to poorer regions or nations that have long lacked that hugely important type of energy. Solar voltaic designer Walt Ratterman has created solar energy systems for people in several parts of the developing world, among them Nicaragua, Myanmar, Thailand, and Rwanda. In the book *Careers in Renewable Energy*, he states, "Working to give people in the developing world access to electricity is always a two-way street. The people we help have so much to gain by improving their access to education, health care, additional work opportunities, and much more. But we gain as much or more from the experience."

How Do You Become a Solar Voltaic Designer?

Education

Partly because solar designers are in increasingly high demand in today's rapidly expanding green energy market, candidates for existing jobs face some stiff competition. It is not unusual, therefore, for the candidate with the most extensive education to fill a given job opening. That education almost always includes four years of college. "For you to start working as a solar energy engineer, you need at least a bachelor's degree in mechanical or electrical engineering or a related field," says Gordon Smith, an engineer who specializes in green energy technologies, in *Solar Thermal Magazine*. The college or university should be accredited by the Accreditation Board of Engineering and Technology, or ABET.

Such four-year programs are the minimum for getting a good job in the solar industry. Experts in the field recommend that when possible, the would-be solar designer should take as many courses related to solar power as possible. The widely respected Peterson's manual *Green Careers in Energy* points out, "Some four-year schools have arrangements with community colleges or liberal arts colleges that allow students to spend two or three years at the initial school and transfer [to the four-year school] for the last two years to complete their engineering degree."

There are also a number of educational opportunities available for people to study solar and related green energy fields either before or after acquiring a degree in engineering. Individual courses and entire programs of courses are offered at various technical and trade schools, community colleges, adult night schools, and in the military. Most of these programs require a high school diploma (or the equivalent) and solid reading and math skills.

Certification and Licensing

All fifty US states, along with the District of Columbia, require that all engineers who deal directly with the public be licensed. Once licensed, a person bears the title Professional Engineer. To get the license, individuals must show proof that they graduated from a four-year college program in engineering accredited by ABET.

Candidates for a license also have to pass a state exam. In addition, they must have one to four years of experience working in some capacity for a company that makes and/or installs solar energy equipment. Most states recognize engineering licenses obtained in other states as long as the requirements are more or less the same.

Internships

Depending on the situation, the work a candidate does to get his or her license may pay a minimal salary or be strictly volunteer in nature. Some companies label such work an internship. "As you go through your college education," Smith urges, "ensure that you undertake an internship related to solar energy engineering." Such internships, he adds, "are offered in most solar energy firms."

Skills and Personality

To be an effective solar designer, one must first possess an aptitude for and strong interest in science and math. One must also be adept at problem solving and troubleshooting and have better-than-average computer skills, as well as the ability to produce clear, concise electrical and mechanical drawings. Other, more specific skills that are handy include knowledge of and/or experience with power conversion equipment, thermodynamics and the workings of photovoltaic cells and panels, semiconductors and spectrometers, and solar energy industry standards.

On the Job

Employers

A number of different types of companies employ solar designers. Among them are manufacturers of solar panels and other solar equipment. Such firms task designers with creating new versions of solar equipment, overcoming technical problems in older equipment, making both old and new equipment more efficient and safer to use, and in some cases developing new computer software for creating and maintaining solar energy systems. Solar energy contractors who specialize in creating and installing such systems also hire solar designers, as do some construction companies that include solar energy systems in the structures they build.

Working Conditions

Solar designers spend much of their time working indoors in offices, where they enter their calculations into computers, complete their system designs, construct diagrams and blueprints for the installers, and so forth. However, solar designers do sometimes visit construction sites, solar arrays, and/or other kinds of work sites. There they make or recheck calculations or supervise the installation of solar equipment. The conditions on the work sites tend to be fairly safe, although designers must be wary of the same dangers common to all construction sites, including being hit by falling debris and stepping on nails.

Earnings

The salary for solar designers varies from state to state and also depends on the person's level of experience. In 2017 those starting out or having minimal experience in the field earned as little as $64,000 per year. Those who had a few years or more of experience were paid at rates competitive with other kinds of engineers. Solar designers received wages on a par with biomedical engineers, who made an annual average of $90,000 to $91,000. Solar designers did make more in a few regions of the country. The best paying of all was the District of Columbia, where those with a lot of experience made as much as $116,000.

Opportunities for Advancement

As solar designers steadily become more experienced, it is common for them to advance in one way or another in the company they work for. They may come to manage the office or even the entire firm, for instance. In a large company, they may supervise a team of engineers and installers, including when on-site installation takes place.

What Is the Future Outlook for Solar Voltaic Designers?

Fortunately for those interested in a career in solar design, in 2017 the outlook for future work was extremely positive. The Bureau of Labor Statistics projected an impressive average growth rate of 7 percent to 13 percent for that profession for several years to come. Indeed, says science writer Gregory McNamee in his book *Careers in Renewable Energy*, the near future will witness many new openings for solar designers. Demand for them "is expected to exceed supply considerably over at least the next decade, and though the entry-level qualifications are rigorous, the rewards are substantial."

Roger Duncan, former manager of a large Texas green energy company, agrees. Current and future growth rates of the solar energy industry can be partially measured, he points out, by the number of watts that solar farms and other solar facilities put out each day. "We've gotten out of the kilowatt [one thousand watts] range," he states, "and the megawatt [1 million watts]. And now we're in the hundreds of megawatts being developed. You'll see large growth in the solar industry over the next decade."

American Solar Energy Society (ASES)
2400 Central Ave., Suite A
Boulder, CO 80301
e-mail: info@ases.org
website: www.ases.org

Founded in 1954, ASES has more than ten thousand members across the United States. They promote and work toward a completely sustainable energy future for the nation and world. Also, the ASES website is a frequent meeting place for professional solar designers from around the country and beyond.

International Renewable Energy Agency (IRENA)
Masdar City
PO Box 236
Abu Dhabi, United Arab Emirates
website: www.irena.org

IRENA defines itself as an organization that supports nations that are transitioning to a the widespread use of renewable energy, and provides a major platform for international cooperation, and a storage facility for technology-related and financial information on renewable energy.

Smart Electric Power Alliance (SEPA)
1220 Nineteenth St. NW, Suite 800
Washington, DC 20036
website: www.solarelectricpower.org

SEPA conducts research in improving and expanding renewable energy systems, including solar. The group regularly publishes booklets and other information sources describing its work and the solar and renewable industries in general.

Solar Voltaic Installer

What Does a Solar Voltaic Installer Do?

Solar voltaic installer is only one of several titles for this job. Depending on the country, region, or even the individual company, the position can also be called solar photovoltaic installer, solar installer technician, solar installation technician commercial, solar field service technician, or more simply, solar technician or solar installer.

The particular name of the job aside, what a solar installer does depends on the setting in which he or she works. Some solar installers spend much of their time on solar farms, large arrays of solar panels located in open, flat areas. In the United States these are most often located in the Southwest or other regions where sunlight is abundant year round or nearly so. On a solar farm, an installer sets up new solar panels by following the diagrams or blueprints provided by a solar designer. Solar installers also conduct repairs on existing panels and otherwise maintain the site.

Most solar installers, however, work for individual companies that do both commercial and residential installations of solar equipment and systems. Commercial installations usually consist of setting up solar panels or hot water systems for factories or other large businesses. In contrast, residential installations typically involve providing such systems for individual homes. Solar installer Kristin Underwood says on the TreeHugger website, "Personally, I prefer residential jobs because they only last a few days, you work directly with homeowners, and you have more room for creativity on the job."

Whether working in commercial or residential settings, installers have numerous fairly standard duties to perform. One of the chief ones, as is also the case for installers who work on solar farms, is assembling solar panels by following diagrams and other instructions provided by solar designers. This includes setting up the support structures for the

Solar voltaic installers make sure solar panels are properly placed for maximum solar energy intake. Some installers specialize in commercial installations; others work mainly on residential projects, and still others do both.

panels. The supports consist of metal or plastic pipes, struts, brackets, and other similar materials. Although this assembly follows standard designs and methods, inevitably individual jobs often require installers to make alterations dictated by specific on-site variations. In addition to assembling solar panels and their supports, installers often must apply weather-sealing materials to keep the equipment from corroding.

When a job involves solar water heating systems, installers have to determine the best locations for the tanks. They also must connect the tanks to or disconnect them from power sources. Other typical duties in such cases include filling the tanks and checking for leaks, identifying potential plumbing and/or electrical problems, installing circulating pumps and/or heat exchangers where necessary, and adding ultraviolet radiation protection to keep those high-energy rays from damaging the various plumbing components.

As is true of solar panel installation, assembling such solar heating systems in commercial or residential settings is normally done by following blueprints created by the company's solar designer. Still, the installers almost always encounter local variations in houses and larger buildings that are not foreseen in those instructions. So an installer must be ready to improvise to one degree or another in order to make the new system work.

This improvisational aspect of the job is actually seen as a plus by many solar installers. "Every job is different," Underwood points out. That means

> that some jobs can be really challenging. [I] have found that the most challenging jobs usually leave you with a "YEEEESSS!! Take That!" feeling when you finally accomplish what felt like an impossible task. Also, homeowners are always excited to see you and even more excited to see their system on and working. Having a job where you are always congratulated for "finishing" the job and a job well done is really great. Also, all the installers I know take pride in their job, not just because it takes skill and finesse to do the job, but also because we know we are doing something important. [Our work] makes a difference and is vital to our energy future and economy. That is quite a responsibility.

How Do You Become a Solar Voltaic Installer?

Education

The amount of education and training required for solar installers depends on whether the job opening is for an entry-level position or one that requires experience. This is because installers include both beginners and advanced workers. For beginners—typically labeled helpers, laborers, or apprentices—only a high school diploma (or its equivalent) is required. In such cases it is understood that the applicant will learn while on the job.

For job openings for more advanced installers, some classroom instruction beyond a high school diploma is generally called for. This extra education might entail taking one or more courses at a community college. As Underwood tells it:

> More and more solar and renewable energy training courses are offered in community colleges these days around the country and some even have practical or hands-on applications in the course. If you're thinking about getting in the field but can't find a solar course near you, it wouldn't hurt to take an intro electrical course at your local community college. Knowing what you can and can't do when it comes to electricity just might save your life on the job, plus would give you an edge over applicants that just have basic work experience.

Beginners in solar installation can also take courses at a technical or trade school. Alternately, some solar and other utility companies offer in-house training programs of their own to novices in the trade.

Certification and Licensing

At present certification and/or licensing is voluntary for solar installers in the United States. However, some states are considering requiring it. Also, some installers decide to voluntarily become certified because they feel it improves their chances of finding a good job. For those who take that route, the North American Board of Certified Energy Practitioners provides the certification. In a different vein, some solar installers had licenses as general contractors or electricians before entering the solar field.

Apprenticeships

As a rule, people do not volunteer to work as solar installers—that is, offer to work with no pay. But they do frequently work as apprentices in order to learn the trade. Apprenticeships are most often offered by solar energy companies and some related trade organizations. For a minimal amount of pay, the apprentice learns on the job by working alongside one or more seasoned professionals. Depending on the beginner and his or her personal background and situation, an apprenticeship typically lasts one to three years.

Skills and Personality

It is best for a would-be solar installer to possess certain natural inclinations and skills in order to excel at the job. For example, he or she should be adept at using a variety of tools—mechanical, measuring, and electronic alike. That includes the repair and maintenance of those devices. Having basic math skills is another plus.

Also useful is the ability to troubleshoot and solve problems, which are bound to arise on any commercial or residential job, as well as on a solar farm. Part of that problem-solving capacity is an excellent aptitude for visualization—the talent to see in one's mind's eye how something will look after it is moved around or when its parts are assembled or rearranged.

In addition, the applicant for a solar installer's job should feel fairly comfortable with frequent exposure to high places. Installing equipment on rooftops or while standing on ladders is common in the profession. This also means that an appreciation for safety issues is an integral facet of the job.

On the Job

Employers

In the rapidly expanding solar energy industry, a number of different types of employers hire solar installers. Solar farms, solar energy companies, and solar thermal contractors (those who specialize in solar heating systems) all require installers. In addition, some large general construction companies that often include solar electricity in their buildings hire one or more solar installers when needed.

Working Conditions

Solar installers spend the bulk of their time outdoors, although some of their work—especially that related to solar heating systems—occurs indoors. Because working on roofs and other elevated places is common, some potential dangers are involved, and a fair amount of time each day is devoted to taking proper safety precautions. This often includes using a harness and anchor system to ensure that a worker does not fall from a roof or ladder. Also, sometimes parts of a roof must be reinforced to keep installers from breaking through into a structure's upper story. In addition, an installer must be extremely careful to avoid dropping and breaking the solar panels, which weigh up to 40 pounds (18 kg) each and are very expensive to replace.

Another possible aspect of the job is sometimes being away from home. A number of solar companies take on jobs in cities far from where its installers live, so periodic traveling can be involved. According to Underwood:

> We travel and spend more time out of town than when I first started. Since jobs are located wherever a contract is signed, and sales guys are spread out all over the state in order to cover the market, jobs are spread out much further apart these days. This means a lot of time in the car driving around traveling and a lot of time living out of a suitcase in hotels. For techs that are young (and single) this is not as much of a problem (though it definitely cuts into your social life), but for married folks this is something to consider as it means lots of time away from family and can be hard on couples with small children.

Earnings

In 2016–2017 most solar installers in the United States earned in the range of $18 to $19 per hour, or about $39,240 per year. Salaries somewhat less or more than that were reported in a few states and individual regions.

Opportunities for Advancement

It is very common for novice solar installers to enter a company and work as beginners or apprentices until they are better trained and more seasoned in the trade. In time, an ambitious installer typically advances in the company and may even become a shift supervisor. Now and then a particularly career-oriented installer will decide to go back to school long enough to advance to the rank of solar designer. (In some cases company managers may suggest the person do this and help him or her with tuition money or other aid and incentives.)

What Is the Future Outlook for Solar Voltaic Installers?

Future job prospects for solar installers in the United States and most other parts of the world are extremely optimistic. The Bureau of Labor Statistics estimates that the solar industry will grow by 14 percent to 20 percent between 2017 and 2024, and further growth is expected in following years. Solar installers will remain at the core of the industry as it grows. In 2015, the Massachusetts Institute of Technology (MIT) published a major study on solar energy's future. It concluded that the generation of solar electricity has tremendous growth potential at least up to the year 2050.

Find Out More

Florida Solar Energy Center
1679 Clearlake Rd.
Cocoa, FL 32922
website: www.fsec.ucf.edu

Florida Solar Energy Center's mission is to conduct extensive research into developing energy technologies that enhance Florida's and the nation's economy and environment, while at the same time creating more jobs for solar installers and other solar workers. The center also seeks to educate the public, students, and practitioners on the results of its ongoing research.

Solar Energy Industries Association (SEIA)
600 Fourteenth St. NW, Suite 400
Washington, DC 20005
e-mail: info@seia.org
website: www.seia.org

SEIA is a major US trade association for the solar industry. It represents numerous companies and community organizations that promote, manufacture, install, and support the development of solar energy. SEIA says that it works with around one thousand companies to champion the use of clean, affordable solar energy in America.

Solar Living Institute (SLI)
13771 S. Highway 101
PO Box 836
Hopland, CA 95449
e-mail: sli@solarliving.org
website: www.solarliving.org

SLI is a nonprofit educational organization that provides classes in solar training and practices for solar installers and other solar workers. Since 1998 SLI has been offering professional solar training taught by experienced practitioners who bring years of real-world knowledge to the classroom.

Wind Turbine Technician

What Does a Wind Turbine Technician Do?

Wind turbine technician is only one of several job titles for this up-and-coming career. Different regions, as well as individual companies, have their preferences for the name of the position, which can include wind turbine services technician, wind services technician, senior wind plant technician, and lead wind technician.

Whatever someone may call this position, in 2016 it became far and away the fastest-growing job in the United States. Part of the reason for this is that the wind energy industry is growing rapidly. Also, the job itself appeals to some people—both male and female—because it combines a certain amount of technical knowledge with some physical challenges. In addition, a number of novices at the job, as well as veterans, express a degree of satisfaction in knowing that they are making a positive difference in the world by helping

A wind turbine technician makes sure a newly installed turbine is operating according to specifications. People who work in this fast-growing occupation must be able to work at great heights in order to clean and maintain turbines and blades.

promote green energy for both current society and humanity's future. According to a wind energy professional on the website of Wind Turbine Technicians, an industry association, "Today, wind turbines are appearing all over the country. You can see them stretching into the skyline of big cities as well as erected out in the countryside of smaller towns and rural areas. They are providing much-needed natural, sustainable energy that will help make the earth a healthier, more cost efficient place to live in the future."

Wind turbine technicians typically work on, as well as inside, those towering windmill-like turbines increasingly seen in both cities and the countryside. Part of the work entails maintaining and cleaning the turbines, including their blades, the inner mechanisms, and the towers themselves. Often involved are duties such as assisting in the assembly of wind turbines, either on wind farms or commercial or private properties; starting, stopping, and restarting the generators that run the turbines; changing filters and other parts on a regular schedule; testing electrical and hydraulic systems using standard testing equipment; collecting on-site data for use in research and analysis; maintaining inventories of the many special tools required for this special job; and helping train less experienced technicians, as on-the-job-training is an integral part of the wind energy industry.

In a typical day for a wind turbine technician, he or she wakes up "before the sun, grabs something to eat, and hits the road," a veteran technician explains on the Wind Turbine Technicians website. Then he or she usually proceeds to the company headquarters. There, the veteran technician says, "you will have a meeting with the whole crew, typically around 7 a.m. You will be grouped into teams as necessary, usually at least three-person teams. Your team will be assigned a specific job task for that day, which can range from scheduled maintenance to repairing unexpected failures, typically working on one turbine per day."

Reaching the turbine scheduled for servicing, the technicians face the daunting daily duty of the morning climb to the top. This can be "physically hard," the veteran technician admits. "Have you ever climbed a 26 story ladder?" he asks. "If you become a wind turbine technician you will. Do you deal well with heights? You absolutely cannot have a fear of heights in this job."

At the ladder's top, the technicians reach the hatch, the small door that leads them inside the housing of the enormous machinery that moves when the giant blades spin. Entering the hatch, the workers begin addressing the items on their daily work order, which might include cleaning, repair, troubleshooting, or simply general servicing. In most cases the technicians bring their lunch with them and eat it inside the housing.

How Do You Become a Wind Turbine Technician?

Education

Some wind energy companies will hire a beginner in the field who has only a high school diploma. That situation is steadily changing, however, as the wind industry expands. More and more employers are asking for applicants to have an associate's degree—that is, a diploma from a two-year college program that has at least some courses dealing with the workings, maintenance, and repair of wind turbines. There should also be instruction in basic safety skills required for working around wind turbines. Furthermore, the applicant should make sure that the school he or she chooses is reputable and has instructors who are well-trained in the wind energy field. The number of US community colleges that offer this type of program is growing each year.

In addition to community colleges, some technical and trade schools offer education in wind energy, including how to work on wind turbines. Still more knowledge and training can be obtained on the job. Many wind energy companies offer on-the-job training, as do wind energy trade associations and local unions.

Certification and Licensing

Wind turbine technicians are not yet required to be certified or licensed, in part because the wind energy industry is fairly new compared to traditional energy-producing industries. That situation is steadily changing, however. Although certification is not mandatory, more and more experts recommend that beginners in the field consider it. Having certification or a license can make a person more employable because it shows that he or she is serious, committed, professional, and possesses a certain level of knowledge. The North American Board of Certified Energy Practitioners offers a certificate for wind energy technicians who pass an exam on wind energy technology.

Apprenticeships

Apprenticeships in wind energy jobs, including turbine technicians, are widely available in the industry. Almost all the major wind energy companies offer them. In part this is because company owners and managers want to ensure that all their employees follow company rules, methods, and standards. Also, the industry's ongoing rapid expansion is a factor. According to a spokesperson for Wind Turbine Technicians, "In some states, entry-level wind turbine technician positions are being filled by students who have yet to graduate from their training programs. They are being sought out by companies implementing massive wind turbine programs because the industry is growing so quickly."

Skills and Personality

To be hired for and maintain good-paying jobs as wind turbine technicians, applicants need a number of skills and personal attributes. First, they must have certain physical qualities that not all people possess. They need to be physically fit and have a modest amount of upper-body strength, for example, because climbing up and down ladders ten, twenty, or more stories high is often a daily reality of the job. Also, applicants must be comfortable with heights. Put simply, a person with acrophobia—fear of heights—would be unable to discharge his or her typical duties in a turbine hatch sometimes situated more than 300 feet (91 meters) above the ground.

Wind turbine technicians also need to be good at following directions. Their work is highly technical and detailed, and workers frequently must rely on mechanical diagrams, along with written instructions. Teamwork and good communication skills are also essential for the job. "Wind turbine technicians must be able to work in harmony with others while still working independently as needed," an experienced turbine technician explains on the Wind Turbine Technicians website. "Clear communication is essential to make sure all duties of the job are being completed on schedule."

On the Job

Employers

Most job openings for wind turbine technicians are posted by either wind energy companies that construct wind farms, the farms themselves, or independent wind energy firms hired to do maintenance and repair.

Working Conditions

Almost all of a wind turbine technician's workday is spent outdoors, and a fair proportion of it happens at the top of a towering turbine. One positive attraction of the job for some people is what they describe as a sort of sense of wonder working so high up in such an enormous and unique structure. Heather Jordan, a reporter for a Michigan newspaper, was allowed to climb to the top of a turbine in that state. Entranced, she later wrote on the MLive website about being inside the huge mechanism spun by the turbine's blades at a height of "about 280 feet off the ground." Jordan continues, "Two hatches in the ceiling allow natural light to shine in. The blades that spin in the wind are about 165 feet long, a little longer than a football field is wide. Climb another ladder, open a hatch and pop your head out for a fantastic view of the wind farm stretching for miles all around, a patchwork landscape dotted with white turbines and miniature red barns."

On the flip side of this positive aspect of the job is that when one works so high up, often in the open, a concern for safety is absolutely essential at all times. Indeed, even those technicians who are not afraid of heights must be constantly safety conscious. Working on giant wind turbines is inherently dangerous, in part because on rare occasions mechanical failures, including collapses of the support towers, occur. Human error is also a factor in the yearly death toll attributed to the job.

To date, the wind energy industry has not regularly released figures for deaths and injuries that happen in and around wind turbines. But a few independent studies suggest that around a dozen wind turbine workers die each year worldwide. The research division of the global media company Forbes reported twelve such fatalities in 2012. (Eight of the deaths were in China's wind industry, the safety standards of which are more lax than those in the United States.)

Earnings

In the United States wind turbine technicians make between about $43,000 and $63,000 per year. The exact salary will depend on factors such as the applicant's training and experience, the economy of the local region, and the policies of the company that employs these workers.

Opportunities for Advancement

There is ample opportunity for advancement in the wind energy industry. If a wind turbine technician performs well in the job, he or she may eventually be considered for the position of team leader. In turn, that might in time lead to a management position. In management, the technician will oversee other technicians and ensure that the turbines the company services run smoothly.

What Is the Future Outlook for Wind Turbine Technicians?

The global wind energy industry is growing rapidly, and new jobs for wind turbine technicians are opening up at an increasing pace. The United States is among the leading nations in this growth. According to the US wind industry's 2016 market report, in that year for the first time in history American wind energy companies employed more than 100,000 people. The total was about 102,500. They maintained more than fifty-two thousand wind turbines, and when almost fifteen thousand full-time wind technicians were hired that year, that position became the country's fastest-growing job.

This positive trend is expected to continue well into the future. Studies released in 2016 by the US Department of Energy and the American Wind Energy Association predict that another forty-six thousand or more US wind energy jobs will be added by 2020. Moreover, rapid growth of the industry and its need for new workers, including wind turbine technicians, is expected to continue at least until 2030 and possibly until 2050.

Find Out More

American Wind Energy Association (AWEA)
1501 M St. NW, Suite 900
Washington, DC 20005
website: www.awea.org

AWEA says that it is the leading national trade association representing the interests of America's wind energy industry. AWEA works to make wind energy as cost-competitive as possible.

WindTurbineTechnicians.net
website: www.windturbinetechnicians.net

This useful website contains information on the skills needed to become a wind turbine technician and the availability of schools and jobs in that occupation.

World Wind Energy Association (WWEA)
Charles-de-Gaulle-Str. 5
53113 Bonn
Germany
website: www.wwindea.org

The WWEA is a worldwide nonprofit organization that supports the global wind industry. It boasts a membership of more than six hundred wind companies and utilities in about one hundred countries. The WWEA strongly promotes the use of wind energy and its associated technologies.

Geothermal Technician

At a Glance

Geothermal Technician

Minimum Educational Requirements

High school diploma for entry level

Personal Qualities

Mechanically inclined, good with tools, solid work ethic

Certification and Licensing

Mostly voluntary, but required in some states

Working Conditions

Can be indoors or outdoors, depending on the job

Salary

About $67,000 per year for highly experienced workers; much less for entry level

Number of Jobs

About 5,800 people in the geothermal industry in the United States in 2017*

Future Job Outlook

Steady growth expected

*This number includes geothermal technicians.

What Does a Geothermal Technician Do?

Depending on which country or state they work in or the individual company that employs them, geothermal technicians may also be called geothermal energy technicians, geothermal installers, geothermal field technicians, geothermal equipment operators, or geothermal construction workers. Along with geothermal engineers and other specialized workers, geothermal technicians are part of an industry that taps into the enormous amount of ever-present heat that exists beneath Earth's surface. As the Geothermal Energy Association points out, "The constant flow of heat from the Earth ensures an inexhaustible and essentially limitless supply of energy for billions of years to come."

Essentially specially trained and skilled manual laborers, geothermal technicians are in many ways the mainstay of the geothermal energy

A geothermal technician works on pumps at a geothermal power plant. These technicians operate, maintain, and repair pumps, pipes, and other equipment to ensure smooth and continuous operation.

industry. They usually carry out the plans and follow the instructions of engineers and other highly educated scientists who design geothermal equipment and facilities. All of these workers may, at one time or another, be involved in one of the three main areas of geothermal energy production. The first consists of tapping into reservoirs of underground hot water and transporting it directly to a city for use by its residents. In the second geothermal subindustry, workers use a device called a ground source heat pump to provide heat and/or air-conditioning for a house or other individual structure. Workers in the third major area of geothermal energy production use heat from the planet's interior to generate electricity.

In the first kind of geothermal energy production, which brings underground hot water to a town or city, geothermal technicians operate, maintain, and/or repair the system's pipes and other equipment. They may also reposition or expand existing networks of pipes as needed. Also, some technicians monitor the system and report changes or irregularities to their supervisors.

Geothermal technicians who install ground source heat pumps for houses and other individual buildings have a wide range of possible duties. First, they dig a trench in the ground near the target structure and within the trench install the appropriate pipes and coils that will absorb heat from underground. Having embedded that section of the heat pump system, the technicians install the necessary pipes and ducts in the nearby structure and make sure that those elements connect properly with the equipment in the trench. Then they backfill the trench. After general installation is complete, the technicians perform pressure, flow, and other kinds of tests to ensure that the system is performing properly.

Installing such heat pump systems involves a fair amount of overlap with other construction-related and technology-oriented jobs. For example, geothermal technicians often must disconnect and later reconnect electrical wiring that is adjacent to or in the way of the heating pipes and ducts. In the words of science writer Gregory McNamee in his book *Careers in Renewable Energy*:

> The direct-use technologies employed by geothermal energy require workers trained in heating and air-conditioning systems, as well as in the building trades. The interface between geothermal energy and electrical systems requires electrical technicians, electricians, electrical machinists, welders, mechanics, and other skilled workers. [Also], mechanical engineers, geologists, drilling crews, and heating, ventilation, and air-conditioning contractors are needed to manufacture and install geothermal heat pumps.

Geothermal companies do not hire separate professional plumbers, electricians, and mechanics for every job. So the geothermal technicians often end up performing various aspects of those jobs. That makes them what is known as jacks-of-all-trades.

In the third area of geothermal energy production—making electricity in geothermal power plants—technicians are regularly involved in monitoring and repairing power plant equipment. That equipment typically includes electronic devices of various kinds. The technicians also make sure that safety regulations are followed properly. In addition, they prepare logs, reports, and other documents describing system maintenance and submit these to the plant managers.

How Do You Become a Geothermal Technician?

Education

Most geothermal energy companies and power plants require beginners in the field to have no more than a high school diploma. It is widely understood in the industry that novice geothermal technicians will learn a great deal while on the job. Nevertheless, these workers are encouraged to get extra training when possible, especially in related areas such as electrical, plumbing, and mechanical disciplines. Courses in these areas are readily available in community colleges, trade schools, and even online technical schools. As a rule of thumb, the more educated a technician becomes, the more employable he or she becomes.

Certification and Licensing

No certification or licensing is currently required for beginner geothermal technicians. However, some US states and cities either recommend or demand that those technicians who install ground source heat pumps acquire licenses as plumbers, electricians, or ventilation and air-conditioning installers, depending on the situation. This is because of the considerable overlap in duties and skills that geothermal technicians have with those other professions. The geothermal training company HeatSpring offers a prep course for a professional geothermal certificate, along with the certificate itself.

Apprenticeships

Apprenticeships are routine and widespread throughout the geothermal energy industry. In fact, many geothermal technicians begin as apprentices and learn much of their trade by working alongside more experienced technicians. In part this tradition mirrors the strong apprenticeship traditions of workers in related fields, including electricians and plumbers. According to the Bureau of Labor Statistics, these apprenticeship programs often last three or four years.

Skills and Personality

Like other workers in the geothermal industry and individuals in other green energy industries, geothermal technicians tend to be mechanically inclined. They enjoy both working with tools and finding solutions to challenging technical problems. They should be in good physical shape as well, because the job entails regularly lifting heavy objects, climbing ladders, digging trenches, and other taxing duties. Geothermal technicians also tend to be hard workers with sound work ethics. Those without these qualities usually do not last long in the job.

On the Job

Employers

Some geothermal technicians are employed by large-scale power plants that create electricity using steam produced by underground heat sources. Because those sources are located in relatively few places around the United States and the world in general, opportunities for these jobs are also limited to the specific, isolated areas in question. In contrast, companies that install ground source heat pumps can be found all over the country and in many other nations as well. Those firms employ the bulk of geothermal technicians.

Working Conditions

The typical workday for geothermal technicians takes them outside for a while, then inside for an hour or two, and after that outside again. It can vary a lot from job to job and from one day to another. There is also usually a certain amount of driving involved to get to work sites on the far side of town or in neighboring communities.

Working conditions for geothermal technicians are relatively safe as long as they follow all safety regulations to the letter. Because some of those employees inevitably fail to observe all the rules and freak accidents sometimes occur, the industry reports a certain number of accidents, some of them serious, each year. Falls from ladders or into open trenches occur, for example, as do shocks from touching electrical wires without proper safety precautions.

Another potential danger consists of noxious fumes that sometimes rise from underground chambers that have been exposed by geothermal drilling. In one case, a worker was standing next to a drilling shaft when a plume of poisonous hydrogen sulfide arose. Smelling the gas, he ran, but it was too late and he collapsed not far from the shaft. Fortunately for him, he recovered.

The most common injuries that geothermal technicians sustain are burns caused by exposure to scalding water. In 2009, for example, a worker at California's Terra-Gen Operating Company suffered serious burns to his body. The company's report of the incident stated in part that he

> observed a leak of 150°–160° Fahrenheit geothermal water coming from a temporary diesel engine powered pump and piping system at a collection pond. He shut off the diesel engine of one of the five temporary pumps at the site, then turned around to walk away. After rotating his body he fell into a pool of the heated water. The [company's] emergency action plan was implemented [and] the worker was airlifted to [a regional medical center] to receive treatment.

Earnings

Salaries for geothermal technicians vary widely, depending on the country and state they work in and the policies of the companies that employ them. A worker's level of training and experience are also factors. An entry-level technician, often an apprentice, can earn as little as $22,000 per year. Top-end technicians with several years of experience can make between $63,000 and $67,000 per year, while the average worker makes perhaps $38,000 to $44,000 per year.

Opportunities for Advancement

Usually, geothermal technicians begin as apprentices, assistants, or helpers (depending on what the company chooses to call them). Each beginner works under the supervision of one or more experienced technicians. It is common for a worker to advance through several levels of experience and responsibility. Eventually, the person may become a trainer or even a supervisor.

What Is the Future Outlook for Geothermal Technicians?

Industry experts and outside observers of the industry all agree that the future of geothermal energy in the United States and most other countries is encouraging. The industry has been growing slowly but steadily for several decades, and that growth is expected to continue. Since geothermal technicians in a sense form the manpower backbone of geothermal energy companies, the number of job openings for them should expand as well.

One function of the potential future growth of the industry and its jobs is the growing percentage of electricity a given nation derives from geothermal energy. Some countries have plowed considerable amounts of research and development money into the industry and as a result make a fair proportion of their electricity from geothermal. The Philippines, Iceland, Kenya, and El Salvador, for example, all generate more than 15 percent of their electricity from geothermal energy. That figure is seen to be robust and substantial.

The situation is currently different for the United States, where electrical demand is much larger than in those smaller nations and the use of oil and other fossil fuels to make electricity is still prevalent. Because of these factors, in 2017 geothermal energy produced only about 0.4 percent of US electricity. That percentage is expected to rise steadily in the next several years, however. As McNamee points out, "The Geothermal Energy Association has estimated that with effective federal and state support, as much as 20 percent of the nation's power needs can be met by geothermal energy sources by 2030. [Geothermal] energy is abundant, easily obtained, and, best of all, inexpensive in the long run compared to most other sources of power. That growth means jobs and many opportunities."

Find Out More

Geothermal Energy Association (GEA)
209 Pennsylvania Ave. SE
Washington, DC 20003
website: www.geo-energy.org

On its website, the GEA states that it is a trade association made up of several American companies that support the expansion of geothermal energy. Association members have offices in many states, along with several foreign countries.

Geothermal Resources Council (GRC)
PO Box 1350
Davis, CA 95617
e-mail: grc@geothermal.org
website: https://geothermal.org

The GRC is a nonprofit educational association established in 1970. It has more than thirteen hundred member companies and experts in over forty countries. The GRC aims to continually increase its efforts to educate professionals in the international geothermal community.

HeatSpring
PO Box 4120 #65093
Portland, OR 97208
e-mail: support@heatspring.com
website: www.heatspring.com

HeatSpring was established in 2007 at Babson College, in Massachusetts, as an in-person training company for geothermal professionals. The organization has since grown into a technology company that aids the global green energy building community through offering online information and training.

International Geothermal Association (IGA)
Lennershofstr. 140
D-44801 Bochum
Germany
e-mail: iga@hs-bochum.de
website: www.geothermal-energy.org

The IGA, which formed in 1988, is a scientific, educational, and cultural organization that has about five thousand members in over sixty-five countries. Its goals are to encourage research and development in geothermal energy through the publication of scientific and technical information for governmental representatives and the general public.

Hydrologist

Hydrologists are sometimes called by other titles. Among them are hydrologic engineer, dam designer, and manager of hydrolicensing and water resources. Whatever they may be called, hydrologists often work in or study the hydroelectric, or hydropower, industry, which produces electricity from the energy of moving water. Most hydroelectric stations, or plants, are erected beside dams. They pump some of the dam's water into turbines, which power electrical generators. Electricity made this way is currently the most common form of renewable energy in the United States, as well as the world as a whole. In 2016 hydroelectric stations situated in more than 150 countries created roughly 16.4 percent of the planet's electricity.

Because they are water experts, hydrologists are integral to this huge industry and to other industries that utilize large amounts of water. Hydrologists demonstrate how that vital liquid resource can and should be harnessed to make energy, perform other tasks, and remain drinkable. More specifically, hydrologists study how water in various forms moves through the planet's

---

At a Glance
Hydrologist

Minimum Educational Requirements
Bachelor's degree

Personal Qualities
Strong interest in science, enjoy solving problems, detail oriented

Certification and Licensing
License required in some states

Working Conditions
Indoors and outdoors

Salary
About $80,000 per year on average

Number of Jobs
About 7,500 to 8,000 in 2017

Future Job Outlook
Positive, as the hydropower industry will continue to grow

---

environment. They determine how rain, snow, and other types of precipitation affect lakes, rivers, and groundwater levels. Hydrologists also study how water on or below earth's surface evaporates back into the air and from there eventually precipitates back into the oceans or onto the landmasses. In addition, hydrologists analyze how moving water affects the environment and how that resource can be used to produce energy for human consumption.

Most hydrologists belong to one of two main specialties within the profession—groundwater hydrologists and surface water hydrologists. Truity, a company that provides detailed career information, explains on its website:

> Groundwater hydrologists study the water below the Earth's surface. Most groundwater hydrologists focus on the cleanup of groundwater contaminated by spilled chemicals at a factory, an airport, or a gas station. Some groundwater hydrologists focus on water supply and decide the best locations for wells and the amount of water available for pumping. These hydrologists often give advice about the best places to build waste disposal sites to ensure that the waste does not contaminate the groundwater.

In contrast, surface water hydrologists study water found in lakes, ponds, streams, snow packs, and glaciers. They collect detailed data about how fast water accumulates in or flows out of those places and use that information to predict how much water such places will hold in the future. This allows water engineers and managers to decide the best times to either store water in or release water from those places. Surface water hydrologists also try to estimate when floods might occur in a given area and how damaging such events might be. In addition, both kinds of hydrologist frequently create detailed maps that depict the shapes, contours, and depths of various water sources.

To examine those water sources and collect the data needed to make maps and future predictions, hydrologists use a number of advanced instruments and technologies. These include powerful computers and sophisticated software programs that can analyze the often incredibly complex data these scientists collect. Also commonly used are the Global Positioning System, to find the exact locations of water sources, and remote sensing equipment set up at those locations to collect data.

Although all hydrologists know a great deal about water in general, each typically has a specialty. It is not unusual for that person to spend years studying a single, narrow aspect of the hydrosphere (the combined areas below, on, and above earth's surface that contain water). A good example is Ana Barros, a hydrologist who teaches at Duke University. When not teaching, she researches water's effects on climate, with a special emphasis on the role played by clouds and the rain they produce. "Everyone has seen rain and everyone has seen clouds," she says in an interview in the *Journal of Young Investigators*. "There's no magic there. There's this false sense that because it's familiar, you know everything there is to know about it. In reality, it's incredibly challenging. Once you are able to show students the importance of subtle things that people don't normally appreciate, it's fun to see their excitement."

How Do You Become a Hydrologist?

Education

Some companies and government agencies that hire hydrologists accept a bachelor's degree for entry-level applicants. At present, there are few undergraduate programs specifically in hydrology in US colleges and universities. As a result, people interested in becoming hydrologists should get their undergraduate degree in related scientific disciplines, including engineering and geology or other earth sciences.

Increasingly, however, those who hire hydrologists are demanding graduate degrees (at least a master's degree) even for entry-level jobs. A few universities do offer graduate degrees in hydrology. But students attending universities that do not offer them can get their graduate degree in engineering or geology or some other aspect of natural science. Students should make sure to take at least some courses in advanced math, the physical sciences, computer science, the life sciences, statistics, and if possible environmental law. All of those areas of knowledge tend to play parts in a hydrologist's job at one time or another.

Certification and Licensing

Some states require hydrologists to be licensed, and the licenses are issued by state licensing boards. These entities require the applicant to have a certain level of education, possess a certain amount of experience, and take and pass an exam. Exact licensing requirements vary from state to state. If the applicant has a degree in engineering, officially making him or her an engineer, that person *must* be licensed, as all fifty states and the District of Columbia require engineers to be licensed if they directly serve the public.

Licenses aside, certification in hydrology is largely voluntary. But some entry-level hydrologists choose to become certified to help establish their expertise and thereby make them more employable. The American Institute of Hydrology offers a widely respected certification program.

Internships

Internships in hydrology-related areas are provided by the US Geological Survey (USGS), a government agency that studies the nation's landscape and natural resources. The program, which welcomes both undergraduate and graduate students, is also supported by the National Institutes for Water Resources. The interns are paid minimal salaries and are considered employees of the universities they are attending.

In any given internship, the individual concentrates on studying a narrow, particular topic. For instance, of the 2016 USGS interns, Julia Bowe of the University of Wisconsin studied Connecticut's groundwater network, and Isaac Bukoski of East Carolina University studied the water sources of Cape Cod, in southeastern Massachusetts.

Skills and Personality

Hydrologists inevitably possess a strong interest in science, math, or both and easily adapt to newly emerging technologies. They also tend to be detail oriented and enjoy being challenged by a problem that needs solving. In addition, they almost always have a number of so-called soft skills, of which an important one is critical thinking. This ability to choose wise, effective options over unwise, ineffective ones comes in handy when a hydrologist devises a plan to counteract a given threat to a local water supply. Other soft skills that are useful in the job are good verbal communication ability, better-than-average writing ability, and an aptitude for absorbing and analyzing large amounts of technical data.

On the Job

Employers

About 30 percent of US hydrologists work for the federal government, mostly in the USGS and US Department of Defense. Another roughly 20 percent work for state and city agencies, primarily in departments that oversee conservation, forestry, and water resources. Most of the rest of the hydrologists in the United States are employed by private companies, especially engineering and architectural firms and science-oriented companies. Other hydrologists teach and do research at colleges and universities.

Working Conditions

Hydrologists work indoors in offices and laboratories and outdoors in the field. Indoor work for a hydrologist can include conducting experiments and other research in a lab; using computers to study, analyze, and model data; teaching classes and giving lectures in hydrology and related subjects; and writing reports on their research and findings. In the field, hydrologists visit lakes, rivers, beaches, underground caves and mines, glaciers, and other places featuring large amounts of water. There they observe conditions on the ground, collect data and physical samples, and set up long-term monitoring equipment. Periodic travel to diverse parts of the United States and assorted foreign nations can be fairly common in this job.

Earnings

Salaries for hydrologists vary considerably from state to state in the United States and from country to country in the rest of the world. In the United States interns and entry-level hydrologists may earn as little as $25,000 to $40,000 per year. The median annual pay, however, was around $80,000 in 2017, and in a few states top earners were making as much as $120,000 per year, plus benefits.

A hydrologist measures the water content of California's Sierra Nevada snowpack. Some hydrologists work for hydroelectric plants that generate power while others analyze rain and snow in connection with human and environmental needs.

Opportunities for Advancement

Entry-level hydrologists often work as research assistants or lab technicians. Some assist more experienced hydrologists, geologists, or engineers in the field. Over time, as a hydrologist gains experience, he or she may become a project leader, lab manager, or senior researcher.

What Is the Future Outlook for Hydrologists?

Hydropower and federal labor experts predict that job opportunities for hydrologists will grow at least at a modest rate in the next decade. The Bureau of Labor Statistics suggests a 7 percent increase in the number of hydrologists by 2024. That percentage might end up being low if the chaotic effects of climate change on the world's water sources continue to take an increasingly negative toll.

Indeed, global sea levels have already begun to rise as a result of the steady melting of glaciers and polar ice packs. Moreover, as the planet's atmosphere grows warmer, hurricanes are growing more powerful, and the number of severe flooding events in the United States and elsewhere in the world is increasing. Assuming that this trend continues unabated, the existing number of hydrologists will not be enough to properly study and suggest solutions to these problems. On its website, Truity states:

> More hydrologists will be necessary to assess the threats that global climate change poses to local, state, and national water supplies. For example, changes in climate affect the severity and frequency of droughts and floods. Hydrologists are critical to developing comprehensive water management plans that address these and other problems linked to climate change.

Among other areas of concern that will likely increase demand for the services of hydrologists is saving and managing precious water resources in the face of ongoing global population increases. Those increases spur the expansion of construction of new houses, commercial structures, and entire communities. In turn, this expands demand for freshwater. More hydrologists may be needed to study, manage, and assess the possible depletion of existing water resources caused by population growth.

Find Out More

American Institute of Hydrology (AIH)
AIH, c/o Adept
4600 S. Syracuse St., 9th Floor
Denver, CO 80237
website: www.aihydrology.org

The AIH was established to provide professional standards for the certification of hydrologists and others in the hydropower industry and to create a framework for educating professionals in the industry to reach standards of excellence. The AIH is the only nationwide organization that offers certification to qualified professionals in all fields of the hydrological sciences.

American Water Resources Association (AWRA)
PO Box 1626
Middleburg, VA 20118
e-mail: admin@ahydrology.org
website: www.awra.org/web

The vision and mission of the AWRA are to be accepted as the leading association for information exchange among professionals in the hydroelectric industry, to develop educational materials about water resources and related issues, and to support research into water resources and their management.

International Association for Environmental Hydrology (IAEH)
2607 Hopeton Dr.
San Antonio, TX 78230
e-mail: hydroweb@gmail.com
website: www.hydroweb.com

The IAEH's stated mission is to share technical information about hydrology among scientists and, particularly those practicing their trade in developing countries."

National Hydropower Association (NHA)
601 New Jersey Ave. NW, Suite 660
Washington, DC 20001
e-mail: help@hydro.org
website: www.hydro.org

The NHA is a nonprofit national organization established to promote the growth of clean, affordable US hydropower. It seeks to secure hydropower's place as a climate-friendly, renewable, and reliable energy source that serves national environmental, energy, and economic policy objectives.

Biofuels Processing Technician

At a Glance

Biofuels Processing Technician

Minimum Educational Requirements

High school diploma for entry level; associate's degree preferred for more experienced workers

Personal Qualities

Detail oriented, flexible and adaptable, able to cooperate well with fellow workers

Working Conditions

Mostly indoors

Salary

About $55,000 per year for an experienced technician

Number of Jobs

About 131,000 people in the biofuels/biomass industry in the United States in 2017*

Future Job Outlook

Slower growth rate than other green occupations but will continue to supply many jobs each year

*This number includes biofuels processing technicians.

What Does a Biofuels Processing Technician Do?

Depending on the US state or foreign country where he or she works, a biofuels processing technician may be called by one of several other job titles. These include biofuels production operator, biofuels plant operator, biofuels plant technician, and biofuels maintenance technician. The individuals in this occupation are part of a major, steadily growing green energy industry that itself is routinely called by different names. These include the biofuels industry, bioenergy industry, and biomass energy industry. The latter name is based on the fact that the products it makes are manufactured from biomass, the collective term for materials derived from living or recently living plants or animals. Among many others, these include tree branches and stumps, bamboo, grains and corn, vegetable oils, animal fat and other animal-based oils, and municipal wastes.

From these and other biomass sources, the industry creates biofuels—alternative fuels to fossil fuels. Most biofuel is currently classified either as biodiesel or ethanol. Industry leaders and proponents and supporters of biofuels consider these fuels to be superior to traditional gasoline from both environmental and economic standpoints.

Biomass is also burned to generate electricity. To date, the United States has not yet developed a large-scale industry to do this. In 2017, for instance, less than 2 percent of the country's electricity was produced by biomass.

Most of the more than 130,000 US biomass-related jobs, therefore, are concentrated in the areas of research, development, and manufacture of biofuels. Biofuels processing technician is one of the most prevalent and important occupations in both biofuels research facilities and the processing plants that actually make the fuels. Those technicians, often called "operators" in the processing plants, perform many duties in an average week.

One of the technicians' principal tasks is to operate the diverse and complex chemical processing machines that produce the biofuels. The devices in question include centrifuges, large-scale pumps, processors that remove water from the fuels, special settling tanks that allow one substance to settle out from another, and electrical generators to power all the machines.

A processing technician not only operates these devices but also monitors them, all using advanced computers in a control room. Typically he or she watches multiple screens and types in commands on a keyboard to direct the various steps in the fuel-making process. An experienced senior technician at the National Corn-to-Ethanol Research Center (NCERC) in Edwardsville, Illinois, works in the center's control room, where he monitors the facility's many activities. In a 2016 interview on the OwlGuru website, he explained, "We're working in basically the cutting edge of the biofuels industry, so when we're running [at full capacity] we're on shift work—meaning that we're working twenty-four hours a day [divided into three eight-hour shifts]. [I] normally sit in front of these six screens, monitoring our entire process from right here."

From the control room, two, three, or more technicians perform many of the individual, often intricate functions necessary to transform biomass materials into biofuels. Guided by these workers, the computers do numerous liquid volume measurements and other calculations. The technicians also direct their machines to load and mix corn, grains, vegetable oils, animal fats, and other biomass materials with additives that will speed up their breakdown into forms that can be effectively burned to generate energy.

Other biofuels processing technicians at the NCERC and other biofuels facilities work in on-site labs. Each day, they collect biomass and biofuel samples and subject them to routine lab tests. These tests analyze the materials and judge their quality. Still other biofuels processing technicians do direct inspections of tanks, pumps, and other machines and clean that equipment on a regular basis. No less important duties include disposing of waste products, reporting problems to supervisors, and following the facility's safety procedures.

How Do You Become a Biofuels Processing Technician?

Education

For entry-level jobs, biofuels processing technicians usually need only a high school diploma. Much of their training happens on the job. However, a growing number of employers in the industry say they prefer their beginner technicians to have a bit more education beyond high school. Addressing that point, a technician at the NCERC comments on the OwlGuru website, "High school students can go and get an associate's degree, [which is] kind of like your foot in the door to those operator/technician jobs."

An associate's, or two-year, degree in biofuels technology or any field is available at a number of community colleges. Some trade and vocational schools also offer equivalent programs. Some biofuels technicians use their high school diplomas to initially get a job and then go to night school a little at a time to get their associate's degree. That way they do not have to wait until they obtain the degree to begin working.

Internships

In-house, on-the-job training programs (either apprenticeships or internships) are quite common among biofuels employers. The internship the NCERC offers is widely respected in the industry. Its yearly positions are highly coveted because interns can expect to learn a great deal in one of the finest facilities of its kind in the world.

The NCERC internship is called the Operator and Laboratory Technician in Training Program. The positions are part-time and paid (at rates lower than those made by experienced technicians). The program offers hands-on training in the biofuels processing division and labs in the company's main site in Edwardsville, Illinois. On its website, the NCERC describes the program:

> The purpose of the internship is to gain on-the-job training to develop the skills and experience needed to obtain an entry-level position in the process operations technology industry, such as biofuels, petroleum, biotechnology, or chemical manufacturing. The program is designed for recent graduates, nontraditional candidates who are changing careers, or highly qualified students in their final semester of study. The intern benefits by gaining hands-on experience in process operations technology that will make students more highly competitive for positions in the field. [An intern gains] a network of industry and academic contacts [and] access to opportunities for professional development via mentoring and specialized training opportunities.

Skills and Personality

Biofuels technicians regularly deal with advanced computers and numerous different kinds of specialized machines. So having certain skills and personality traits that help one deal with such a working environment is a big plus for beginners in the occupation. Biofuels technicians should be adept at paying close attention to detail; between the equipment and the frequent paperwork a technician produces, it is a very detail-oriented job.

A biofuels technician also needs to be able to use sound judgment in making on-the-spot decisions when a supervisor is not nearby. In addition, technicians in this job routinely work closely with fellow technicians, as well as with supervisors and customers. So better-than-average communication skills are a must. On the OwlGuru website, a technician at the NCERC adds, "You should obviously have your basic math skills, your basic computer skills, as well as your general English and communication skills."

On the Job

Employers

Most biofuels processing technicians work in plants that manufacture biofuels or in biofuels research facilities and the labs within them. However, some large agricultural and biotechnology firms hire a few of these workers to help with specialized projects of various kinds.

Working Conditions

A majority of biofuels technicians work indoors on the main floors of manufacturing plants or in their control rooms or labs. Often the technicians do their jobs in shifts because the average plant operates around the clock. They are expected to switch from one shift to another with fairly short notice if the company asks them to.

Other typical working conditions make certain abilities necessary for technicians. They need to have a minimal amount of upper-body strength, for example, because they often must lift objects weighing 50 pounds (23 kg) or more. They must also be at least somewhat agile. Frequently, they are called on to climb stairs and/or ladders, stoop, kneel, and walk through rooms crowded with machines of all sizes.

Safety is another important issue. In addition to the heavy machinery, which can be dangerous to work with, biofuels technicians often handle chemicals that can either irritate the skin or be noxious to breathe. Hence, these workers routinely wear various kinds of safety equipment, including goggles, gloves, knee pads, and when necessary, face masks. All biofuels companies require new workers to quickly become proficient in all workplace safety procedures.

Earnings

In the United States, entry-level biofuels technicians may earn as little as $25,000 to $35,000 per year, depending on the state, the company, and the worker's level of education and experience. In 2017 the median salary for experienced technicians was about $55,000 per year, and those with the most education and experience made up to $15,000 more in some places.

Opportunities for Advancement

There is considerable room for advancement in the biofuels industry, including for processing technicians. Typically one starts out as an intern or complete novice and learns on the job. As the person gains experience and expertise, he or she may move up to the position of floor supervisor, control room supervisor, or possibly shift supervisor. On occasion a technician eventually rises to the position of plant manager. (The job of biofuels plant manager requires not only a lot of experience but also more education, which the worker may gain by going to night school on and off for several years.)

What Is the Future Outlook for Biofuels Processing Technicians?

Demand for biofuels processing technicians will continue to increase, according to various US government agencies and the biofuels industry itself. This is because the industry is expected to keep growing for several years to come. However, the experts predict, the industry's growth rate will likely remain about 2 percent per year through the year 2020 and possibly somewhat beyond. This rate is slower than the average growth rate for green jobs in general.

Nevertheless, these projections do not factor in a possible surge in the industry's growth in the 2020s and 2030s. If it materializes, that surge will likely be driven by the creation of new kinds of biofuels that a few research labs are already working on. For example, a team of scientists at the University of California–Los Angeles are studying ways to use bacteria and other microscopic germs to make fuels for cars and other machines. The same lab, along with others around the world, is also looking at ways to convert methane gas into a liquid fuel.

If these and other, similar efforts succeed in creating viable new fuels in the near future, the biofuels industry could conceivably expand significantly in the next two or three decades. If that happens, many more biofuels processing technicians will be needed to help run and maintain the new plants that will inevitably be built to keep up with increased demand.

Find Out More

Advanced Biofuels Association (ABFA)
800 Seventeenth St. NW, Suite 1100
Washington, DC 20006
website: www.advancedbiofuelsassociation.com

The ABFA is dedicated to helping the United States move from a fossil fuels–driven economy to an economy that uses little or no carbon. The ABFA's roughly thirty member companies have the skills and knowledge to create fuels that have lower carbon emissions and are renewable, which will also increase the country's energy security.

Biotechnology Industry Organization (BIO)
1201 Maryland Ave. SW, Suite 900
Washington, DC 20024
e-mail: info@bio.org
website: www.bio.org

The BIO is the world's largest trade association representing biotechnology companies, academic institutions, state biotechnology centers, and various other related groups in the United States, along with more than thirty other countries. BIO members take part in the research and development of new industrial and environmental biotechnology products.

National Biodiesel Board (NBB)
605 Clark Ave.
PO Box 104898
Jefferson City, MO 65110
e-mail: info@biodiesel.org
website: http://biodiesel.org

The NBB is the primary national trade association representing the US biodiesel industry. The organization seeks to make US elected leaders aware of new discoveries and developments in the biodiesel industry and how these will affect the country's economy and security.

Renewable Fuels Association (RFA)
425 Third St. SW, Suite 1150
Washington, DC 20024
website: www.ethanolrfa.org

Established in 1981, the RFA has been a major voice of the US ethanol industry. Its many members have a strong commitment to making America cleaner, safer, and more energy independent. The RFA's experienced staff provides comprehensive industry data to Congress, federal and state government agencies, fuel retailers, and the media.

Green Building Construction Manager

At a Glance

Green Building Construction Manager

Minimum Educational Requirements

Bachelor's degree is becoming the standard requirement

Personal Qualities

Mechanically inclined, strong organizational and leadership skills, detail oriented, willingness to work hard and put in long hours

Certification and Licensing

Generally voluntary

Working Conditions

Both indoors and outdoors

Salary Range

About $85,000 to $90,000 or more for those with experience

Number of Jobs

About 2.9 million green construction workers in the United States in 2017*

Future Job Outlook

Rapid growth expected

*This number includes green building construction managers.

What Does a Green Building Construction Manager Do?

In different cities and states, and also depending on the company that hires them, green building construction managers sometimes go by different titles. Among others, these include green building construction area manager, green building construction foreman, green building construction superintendent, green building job site superintendent, and green building general contractor.

Whatever label it may bear, this challenging profession lies at the heart of the green building construction industry. The fastest-growing sector of the construction industry as a whole, both in the United States and abroad, green building is rapidly eclipsing traditional construction methods. In the latter, there is little thought given to how a house or other building might waste energy, water, and other precious resources. Moreover, studies have shown that structures erected in the traditional way tend to waste huge amounts of those resources. According to science writer Gregory McNamee in his book *Careers in Renewable Energy*, "If there's a dripping faucet, it's dripping at a rate of as much as 20 gallons a day, a drop at a time. If the house is drafty, then it can lose the same amount of heat or cooled air through leakage as it would if a window-sized hole was simply punched through a wall and left open to the elements. The loss from little leaks can amount to more than a third of your utility bill, or even more."

The green construction industry, with green construction managers at its forefront, strives to reverse such wasteful practices and build structures that are resource and energy friendly. This approach is not simply less wasteful and better for people's pocketbooks and the nation's economy, it has also in recent years become the wave of the future for new construction in the United States and a number of other countries. In *Careers in Renewable Energy*, Gregory Esau, a green builder in Vancouver, Canada, explains:

> If you're going to be part of the construction business for the next thirty or forty years, then you're going to have to make sustainability and green building a big part of your repertoire. A lot of [cities and towns], for instance, are going carbon-neutral [minimizing the use of fossil fuels], and we're going to have challenges [in] building the buildings, what with all the big machines we have to use! We'll need good people to help us figure out solutions to problems like that, workers who are on what I call a green track.

Leading those "green track workers" are the construction managers who oversee the crews of carpenters, plumbers, electricians, painters, and other tradespersons who create new houses and other structures. Indeed, a green construction manager, or superintendent, is in charge of an entire green construction site. He or she coordinates all design and building procedures. These include selecting, hiring, and supervising the work of the carpenters, plumbers, and others involved. What is more, the construction manager is tasked with ensuring that the overall project is completed on time and within the budget. If the project fails to meet these goals, the manager must answer to his or her boss. Usually, that is either the architect who designed the structure or the construction company's owner.

Besides making sure that the work site runs smoothly and meets its goals, the green construction manager must make certain that all aspects of construction are environmentally friendly. This includes more than making sure the structure itself meets the latest green building codes. It also means eliminating sloppy and wasteful practices on the surrounding site itself. For example, the construction manager might put in place a recycling plan for any unused construction materials or ensure that no chemicals or other hazardous materials enter the soil on the property.

How Do You Become a Green Building Construction Manager?

Education

In the traditional construction industry, which is fast giving way to green building, most construction managers began as carpenters, plumbers, or other experts in the trades. Through years of experience, they moved up in the industry and eventually became managers. That older system is rapidly changing. Today somewhere between 30 percent and 40 percent of green construction managers come to the profession with four-year college degrees. Furthermore, that percentage is expected to quickly grow in the near future because more and more construction companies are demanding better-educated managers. Those college degrees are most often in construction management, construction science, or civil engineering. The American Council for Construction Education provides help in finding accredited four-year and two-year programs in the construction sciences.

Certification and Licensing

Licensing remains largely voluntary for green construction managers. However, some of these individuals come to the job with licenses they acquired when they were master carpenters, electricians, or plumbers. Although certification is also mainly voluntary, increasing numbers of green construction managers are getting certified. In part this is because a growing proportion of employers see certification as a way to ensure that a manger possesses a certain level of training and experience.

The Construction Management Association of America offers certification for junior and senior college students enrolled in programs in the construction sciences. There is also the much coveted Leadership in Energy and Environmental Design (LEED) certification. Developed by the nonprofit US Green Building Council, it is still voluntary. However, some government agencies now require it, and a growing number of states, cities, and towns are considering requiring it. Everblue, which offers courses in green construction, says on its website:

> For construction managers, earning a LEED credential is worth more than simply marketability. This knowledge is directly related to a construction manager's job responsibilities. With the growth of green building in the construction industry, it's a no-brainer that construction managers grow their skill set accordingly. Earning a LEED credential demonstrates a commitment to long-term savings and reduction in energy consumption. These qualities will forever be cherished by building owners and tenants. Nowadays, the preference is for a "green" building, and stakeholders are going to look for the construction teams that can give them what they want.

Apprenticeships

Usually, no internships are available for the occupation of green construction manager itself, as it is a high-level job that one cannot get without several years of experience in some aspect of the construction trades. However, such a manager may have undergone an apprenticeship or internship years earlier when he or she was, perhaps, a beginning electrician, plumber, or carpenter. Many programs of that sort, which often last from two to four years, are offered by large construction companies. Listings of upcoming apprenticeships and internships in the trades are often posted by the National Center for Construction Education & Research.

Skills and Personality

Because many green construction managers start out in jobs in the construction trades, they tend to enjoy and be good at working with tools. It is also common for them to have a strong interest in creating new things from scratch. Extremely important for a candidate for the job to have are a willingness to take charge of and lead others and strong leadership skills.

In addition, the job features numerous weighty responsibilities and rigorous challenges. To meet them, a construction manager must have a great deal of initiative and be used to a lot of hard work and long hours. He or she needs to be dependable as well. After all, on a daily basis dozens, and in some cases hundreds, of workers rely on him or her to be punctual and physically available to guide them in their own duties.

Other skills and traits that are handy for a green construction manager to possess include strong computer skills, including an ability to adapt quickly to new software programs; equally strong attention to detail; being adept at listening to the complaints, suggestions, worries, and ideas of the workers he or she supervises; and displaying the level of critical thinking necessary to sort through and act on the worthiest of those suggestions and ideas.

On the Job

Employers

Green construction managers are typically hired by construction companies of all sizes that have embraced the strategy of building highly energy-efficient structures powered by clean, renewable energy. In addition, sometimes towns and cities bring in green construction managers to run their departments of public works or infrastructure departments. Other municipalities contract with construction companies with proven records, firms that already employ one or more green construction managers. State governments and the federal government also hire construction companies staffed with managers dedicated to green building principles and methods.

Working Conditions

Green building construction managers work both indoors and outdoors, depending on the weekly and daily needs and circumstances of the project at hand. Almost always they work long hours—ten, twelve, or more per day being common. Typical indoor activities include scheduling and attending meetings; preparing contracts, budgets, and reports; and e-mailing and/or phoning materials suppliers.

In contrast, green construction managers often visit the construction sites to determine firsthand how the work is going. The job is generally safe. However, when at a construction site, a manager is no less subject to injuries, including those caused by falling objects. So it is fairly standard for them to wear protective hard hats in those situations.

Earnings

Experienced green construction managers made an average of $85,000 per year in 2017, according to the BLS. Depending on the state, company, and project, beginners made at least $20,000 less. The most experienced and highly paid managers made $150,000 or more.

Opportunities for Advancement

Because they are already high up in the hierarchy of jobs in a typical green construction company, the firm's construction managers most often have minimal opportunities for advancement. Nevertheless, those openings tend to bring with them considerable prestige and salary increases. A promotion to company administrator is possible, for example. In a few cases a construction manager may even rise to the position of head of the company. Some green construction managers form their own small companies. In such a situation the person starts out as the top boss, who doubles as on-site manager for projects the company takes on.

What Is the Future Outlook for Green Building Construction Managers?

The future for green building construction managers is in general a bright one. The Bureau of Labor Statistics (BLS) and other similar organizations predict that the green building industry will expand steadily into the 2020s and 2030s. This will provide members of the construction trades of all kinds with growing opportunities to find jobs. More green construction managers will be needed to organize and oversee all those new workers. The BLS estimates a growth rate of 14 percent to 19 percent for construction managers in the green building industry in 2018 and very likely the decade that follows. This could easily amount to thousands of new jobs for people in that occupation during that period.

Find Out More

American Council for Construction Education (ACCE)
825 W. Bitters Rd., Suite 103
San Antonio, TX 78216
e-mail: acce@acce-hq.org
website: www.acce-hq.org

According to the ACCE, its mission is to provide quality construction education on a global scale. Indeed, among the reasons the organization formed were to improve construction education and to help colleges and universities begin to offer accredited construction education programs.

American Institute of Constructors (AIC)
19 Mantua Rd.
Mount Royal, NJ 08061
e-mail: info@professionalconstructor.org
website: www.professionalconstructor.org

The AIC promotes professionalism and excellence throughout the various related fields of construction. The organization offers the opportunity for construction managers and other industry members to earn professional credentials. To do so, candidates must meet national standards developed by the industry through the Constructor Certification Commission.

Construction Management Association of America (CMAA)
7926 Jones Branch Dr., #800
McLean, VA 22102
e-mail: info@cmaanet.org
website: http://cmaanet.org

The CMAA's mission is to encourage and support the profession of construction management and to promote the hiring of qualified managers for major construction projects. The organization also offers certification for college juniors and seniors planning to become construction managers.

National Center for Construction Education & Research (NCCER)
13614 Progress Blvd.
Alachua, FL 32615
website: www.nccer.org

The mission of the NCCER is to promote a safe, productive, and reliable group of construction professionals. The organization aims to achieve universal recognition within the construction industry and the US government as the foremost provider of training, assessment, certification, and career development for construction professionals, including construction managers.

Radiation Protection Technician

What Does a Radiation Protection Technician Do?

Radiation protection technician is perhaps the most common title for this important job, but by no means the only one. Some others include health physics technician, nuclear chemistry technician, radiation protection specialist, radiochemical technician, and often simply radiation technician.

Whatever a member of this occupation may be called, he or she most often works in facilities that generate excess potentially hazardous radiation. This is often (though not always) associated with the one hundred nuclear power plants in the United States. Those facilities use nuclear fission—the process of releasing energy by splitting atoms—to generate electricity. The technology is considered largely renewable because enough of the mineral used for fuel, uranium, exists to power civilization for many thousands of years.

US nuclear plants and the many other facilities that produce radiation have many built-in safeguards to make sure that this potentially dangerous substance remains under control and does not harm humans or other living creatures. That is where radiation technicians come in. They are the chief safety experts in a typical facility that handles radioactive materials.

In a nuclear plant, for example, a radiation technician's principal duty is to measure and record the level of radiation emitted by the fission process and warn the plant's other employees if radiation levels become too high. Keith Ferdinando is a radiation protection technician at the Brunswick Nuclear Plant located near Southport, South Carolina. He describes his job in an article on the Duke Energy website:

> As a radiation protection technician at Brunswick Nuclear Plant, it is my responsibility to help limit site teammates' radiological exposure, or as we call it, "dose." I'm almost like a police officer; I work to protect people in the plant from radiation. Radiation is an interesting thing; you can't see it. I have to use my knowledge and equipment to help me locate it, as well as brainstorm ways to reduce employees' exposure.

Ferdinando and other radiation technicians have a long list of responsibilities and duties to perform in any given week. First, they must inspect and when necessary service the sensitive radiation detection instruments that are the central focus of their work. These machines have to be calibrated carefully and must be in top working condition at all times. If they are not, the health or even the lives of the plant's employees can be put at risk.

Radiation technicians also deal directly with the plant's radioactive materials. They sometimes collect, examine, and analyze samples of those materials. Following such examinations, the technicians record a wide array of data about the samples and enter it into the plant's extensive computer databases. In addition, when necessary they store samples or package them for disposal. (Usually, employees specially trained in disposal of dangerous materials, *not* the radiation technicians, actually get rid of the spent uranium.)

While carrying out these and other duties, radiation technicians continue to carry out their primary function—monitoring the existing radiation levels inside and directly outside the facility. "I log on to my remote radiological monitoring system on my computer," Ferdinando explains.

> We have remote monitors throughout the site's radiological areas which ensure radiological levels stay normal. These machines are extremely helpful because not only will they alert us if the radiation level exceeds a specific set point, but they also let us know the radiation level of an area before we go in. I also perform surveys of radiological areas where teammates need to work. The surveys I conduct help determine the dose estimate for each job, but it is also a chance for me to reduce radiation levels if necessary in any particular area.

Radiation protection technicians are not only radiation "policemen," as Ferdinando colorfully puts it, but also in a sense radiation "teachers." They sometimes hold seminars in which they teach other plant personnel how to be as safe as possible while doing their various jobs. Technicians like Ferdinando also issue special protective gear to fellow workers who require it and make sure they know how to use that gear correctly.

In addition, radiation technicians are sometimes in a sense radiation "lawyers." At certain times each year, a technician updates his or her knowledge of legal policies, laws, and diverse other regulations. These are periodically formulated by the US Nuclear Regulatory Commission and the states in which nuclear plants are situated.

How Do You Become a Radiation Protection Technician?

Education

If a radiation technician does not work in a nuclear plant, he or she usually needs only a high school diploma to get a job. In such cases the applicant will be expected to learn much of the position's basics while on the job. In contrast, applicants for the same job in nuclear plants now require more preliminary education. An associate's degree (a two-year program) is the standard, and it is recommended that would-be radiation technicians study physics so as to better understand how radiation works. Extra courses that are said to be helpful are environmental science and public health. Radiation technicians who aspire to become the highest-ranking members of the profession—often called "senior" radiation technicians—are expected to get a four-year degree in physics or environmental science.

Wherever the applicant goes to school, taking as many science courses as possible usually pays off later. This is partly because many prospective employers now require the person to take an exam demonstrating the breadth of his or her knowledge in areas related to the occupation. Often employers administer exams prepared by the National Registry of Radiation Protection Technologists.

Certification and Licensing

Although radiation protection technicians are not usually required to be certified, employers look favorably on those who are. This is mainly because certification involves taking a course with the US Department of Labor's Occupational Safety and Health Administration. After passing the course, technicians are more knowledgeable about safety issues in various kinds of facilities in which radiation is produced. Topics covered in the course include emergency response operations; storage, disposal, and/or treatment of hazardous substances; protection against hazardous chemicals and radiation; elimination of hazardous radiation; and the safety of workers who might be exposed to radiation.

Apprenticeships

A good deal of on-the-job training is a standard aspect of the radiation technician occupation. A large proportion of US facilities that generate hazardous wastes, including radiation, offer apprenticeships that may last up to two years.

Skills and Personality

A number of diverse skills and personality traits are associated with the profession, whether the person is an ordinary radiation technician or a senior radiation technician. First, attention to detail is an absolute must. The health and lives of all who work in a technician's home facility are at risk if he or she is careless and makes a mistake that allows the release of radiation or other hazardous wastes. Integrity and dependability are also vital because the other workers put their lives in the technician's hands and need to trust him or her.

Other skills and traits are related to the serious nature and pressures of the job. Several of the occupation's duties can be stressful, complicated, and frustrating at times. So radiation technicians should be able to handle a good deal more stress than average people can. They need to be flexible and able to fairly easily adapt to unexpected situations. In addition, when faced with an emergency, a radiation technician's reaction should be analytical rather than emotional; that is, he or she should put fear aside and immediately evaluate the situation and decide on an effective and safe solution.

Typically, radiation protection technicians also have a fair number of administrative tasks to fulfill in an average week. So skills such as the ability to create detailed schedules and reports in a clear and timely manner are necessary. Other important skills include a strong interest in or inclination for science, a personal facility for working around and with complex machines, good listening skills, and the ability to solve complex problems.

On the Job

Employers

Three principal kinds of employers hire radiation protection technicians. One is a private organization that has one or more labs or other facilities containing equipment that emits radiation. Among these are hospitals, university research labs, various independent research labs, and numerous companies that specialize in industrial processes involving radioactive elements.

The second kind of employer that hires radiation technicians is a construction company building a nuclear plant, factory, hospital, or other facility where radioactive substances will be used. Radiation risks tend to be fairly low on most construction sites; nevertheless, some potential hazards may exist, and these companies usually keep at least one radiation technician on-site as a safety measure.

The remaining radiation technicians take jobs in government agencies and facilities. Among them are US Department of Energy facilities, US Department of Defense facilities, some federal regulatory agencies, and the nation's nuclear plants.

Working Conditions

Radiation protection technicians typically work indoors, although they sometimes inspect the outsides and grounds of buildings for radiation leakage. Most of the radiation technicians in nuclear plants work full time. Because of the nature of the work—with radiation leaks possible at any time of the day and night—some of these individuals have to work night shifts. Similarly, some have to work on weekends and holidays. Some heavy lifting and working at considerable heights is involved as well.

The chief working condition concern of the occupation, of course, is safety. Therefore, these workers must maintain a long list of safety standards at all times. This means frequently having to wear protective equipment. Ferdinando states, "I have to dress in anti-contamination clothing, which is made of plastic, rubber and Orex, a unique water-resistant material. I also wear small dosimeters around my neck that not only read how much radiation I'm receiving, but also the rate at which I am receiving it. [Even though] I have a lot of experience, I'm learning [new facts and procedures] every day."

Earnings

In 2017 the median salary for a radiation technician with a few years of experience ranged from $76,000 to $82,000 per year. A senior radiation technician—with a four-year degree and considerable experience—earned between $99,000 and $105,000.

Opportunities for Advancement

Advancement in the occupation is usually fairly limited. In most cases an ordinary radiation technician *can*, with sufficient experience and training, move up to the job of senior radiation technician. Beyond that, however, to advance further in the nuclear industry, for instance, one would have to go back to school and train for a different job.

What Is the Future Outlook for Radiation Protection Technicians?

Job demand for radiation protection technicians will likely rise in the early 2020s. However, the rate of growth of the occupation will be moderate, according to the Bureau of Labor Statistics and other sources. Demand for the job *could* be higher in the future if the US nuclear power industry were to begin expanding rapidly. But at present, experts see that prospect as unlikely.

Find Out More

American Nuclear Society (ANS)
555 N. Kensington Ave.
La Grange Park, IL 60526
website: www.ans.org

The ANS is a professional organization of scientists, engineers, and other professionals devoted to the peaceful applications of nuclear science and technology. Its eleven thousand members from over forty countries come from diverse technical disciplines ranging from physics and nuclear safety to operations and power.

National Registry of Radiation Protection Technologists (NRRPT)
PO Box 3084
Westerly, RI 02891
e-mail: nrrpt@nrrpt.org
website: www.nrrpt.org

The NRRPT states that its main objective is to promote the education of radiation protection technologists and in the process advance the scientific discipline of health physics. To do this, the NRRPT has created a credentialing exam containing 150 questions.

Nuclear Energy Institute (NEI)
1201 F St. NW, Suite 1100
Washington, DC 20004
e-mail: webmaster@nei.org
website: www.nei.org

The NEI develops policy on key legislative and regulatory issues affecting the nuclear energy industry. In addition, the NEI serves as a unified industry voice before the US Congress, executive branch agencies, and federal regulators, as well as international organizations and venues.

US Nuclear Regulatory Commission (NRC)
Washington, DC 20555-0001
website: www.nrc.gov

The NRC formulates policies and regulations related to the safety of nuclear reactors and the radioactive materials they employ for fuel. Organizations that want to build new reactors must be licensed by the NRC. Officials who work at the four NRC regional offices conduct inspection, enforcement, and emergency response programs for nuclear reactors in the United States.

Interview with a Solar Voltaic Installer

Peter Murphy is a solar photovoltaic installer at SunWind LLC, in Orleans, Massachusetts. He has worked as a solar installer for five years. He answered questions about his career by e-mail.

Q: Why did you become a solar photovoltaic installer?

A: I became a solar installer in a completely opportunistic way. I had worked for a construction company that had partnered with a solar company on a few projects, and at the time, the solar outfit needed workers while the construction company didn't need any workers at that moment in time. I stuck with the solar energy job because it afforded me an opportunity to learn a little bit about other trades such as basic electrical and plumbing (when working on solar thermal installations). It's also nice to know you're contributing, in some small way, to a more sustainably-powered future for our country and for the world as a whole.

Q: Can you describe your typical workday?

A: A typical workday can vary. I've been in the industry for a little over five years, and worked at different solar-oriented companies, ranging from a large corporation with thousands of employees and branches across the country, to a small start-up with just three people (which is my current work situation). A typical workday for an installer can differ greatly depending on the scale and type of company. At a larger company, an installer's work is more narrowly focused and almost completely confined to working on the roof (when doing residential, roof-mounted installs). That includes marking up the layout of a system from a plan set [the blueprints supplied by the solar designer], installing the mounting system (that will hold the solar panels), running conduit and whatever wiring required to tie in to the inverter or existing electrical system, and finally laying down the PV [solar] panels and connecting them and securing them to the mounting system. In addition to these duties and tasks, at a smaller company you might find yourself wearing additional hats—from covering sales and marketing-related tasks; to the clerical-type work of filing permits [with the town in which the installation takes place], system design and budgeting—that is, all the "soft cost" work that is involved in keeping the company operating, of which the installation process is only a small part.

Q: What do you like most and least about your job?

A: I really like the people I work with, which I think is paramount regardless of your profession. And I like working at a small company where I have a very fluid (broad and sometimes changing) job description. That said, I have worked as an installer at companies where the work environment was less agreeable, and the work conditions were, at times, downright unsafe. For instance, when a company asks the installers to work on a roof without all the sufficient safety equipment. As a solar installer, you face the combined risks of working on a roof, working in extreme conditions (you are almost always going to be working in an area of maximum exposure to the sun), working with electricity, which can be dangerous if not handled correctly, and sometimes handling hazardous substances. Some of these risks are unavoidable, but it's important to have an employer that values your personal safety over profit.

Q: What personal qualities do you find most valuable for this type of work?

A: I wouldn't say there is any particular personal trait that is most valuable aside from a general good work ethic and maybe a tolerance for the occasionally grueling work conditions I've mentioned. That, and also don't be too afraid of heights!

Q: What advice do you have for students who might be interested in this career?

A: I think having a strong grasp of the electrical side of things is extremely useful, and knowing how to troubleshoot a system when things go wrong (which I think is more of a practical skill gained from experience, or from working with someone who is experienced, than it is theoretical knowledge), but also having an idea of best roofing practices, which is sometimes overlooked because it's not always obvious that a roof isn't weather-tight until it rains. So study up, but also apprentice as much as you can.

Other Jobs in Renewable Energy

Agricultural engineer
Atmospheric scientist
Biomass production manager
Civil engineer
Computer programmer
Computer technician
Electric power line installer
Environmental engineer
Fuel cell engineer
Geophysicist
Geothermal electrician
Geothermal heat pump engineer
Geothermal marketing and sales
    director
Green building architect
Green building contractor
Green building project analyst
Hydraulic engineer
Hydraulic executive
Hydraulic marketing and sales
    director
Hydroelectric power technician

Hydrogen energy process
    manager
Meteorologist
Nuclear energy business
    manager
Nuclear engineer
Nuclear physicist
Nuclear reactor operator
Renewable energy research
    scientist
Smart grid engineer
Solar energy researcher
Solar executive officer
Solar financial director
Solar marketing and sales
    director
Transportation planner
Wind marketing and sales
    director
Wind turbine engineer
Wind turbine researcher

Editor's note: The US Department of Labor's Bureau of Labor Statistic provides information about hundreds of occupations. The agency's *Occupational Outlook Handbook* describes what these jobs entail, the work environment, education and skill requirements, pay, future outlook, and more. The *Occupational Outlook Handbook* may be accessed online at www.bls.gov/ooh.

Index

About the Author

In addition to his numerous acclaimed volumes on ancient civilizations, historian Don Nardo has published several studies of scientific discoveries and phenomena, including *Sustainable Energy*, *Climate Change*, *Polar Explorations*, *Volcanoes*, and award-winning books on astronomy and space exploration. Nardo also composes and arranges orchestral music. He lives with his wife, Christine, in Massachusetts.